CENGAGE Learning

Drama for Students, Volume 6

Staff

Editorial: David M. Galens, *Editor*. Tim Akers, *Contributing Editor*. James Draper, *Managing Editor*. David Galens and Lynn Koch, *"For Students" Line Coordinators*. Jeffery Chapman, *Programmer/Analyst*.

Research: Victoria B. Cariappa, *Research Manager*. Andrew Guy Malonis, Barbara McNeil, Gary J. Oudersluys, Maureen Richards, and Cheryl L. Warnock, *Research Specialists*. Patricia Tsune Ballard, Wendy K. Festerling, Tamara C. Nott, Tracie A. Richardson, Corrine A. Stocker, and, Robert Whaley, *Research Associates*. Phyllis J. Blackman, Tim Lehnerer, and Patricia L. Love, *Research Assistants*.

Permissions: Maria Franklin, *Permissions Manager*. Kimberly F. Smilay, *Permissions Specialist*. Kelly A. Quin, *Permissions Associate*.

Sandra K. Gore, *Permissions Assistant*.

Graphic Services: Randy Bassett, *Image Database Supervisor*. Robert Duncan and Michael Logusz, *Imaging Specialists*. Pamela A. Reed, *Imaging Coordinator*. Gary Leach, *Macintosh Artist*.

Product Design: Cynthia Baldwin, *Product Design Manager*. Cover Design: Michelle DiMercurio, *Art Director*. Page Design: Pamela A. E. Galbreath, *Senior Art Director*.

Copyright © 1999
The Gale Group
27500 Drake Rd.
Farmington Hills, MI 48331-3535

ISBN 0-7876-2755-0
ISSN 1094-9232
Printed in the United States of America

10 9 8 7 6 5 4 3

Hay Fever

Noel Coward

1925

Introduction

Noel Coward's plays epitomize the sophisticated wit of the era between the two world wars, and *Hay Fever*, a comedy of manners about a family whose theatrical excesses torment a group of unsuspecting visitors, epitomizes the Coward play. Inspired by a weekend he spent at the house of the actor Laurette Taylor, Coward wrote the play in just three days. Upon its 1925 London debut on August 6, it won praise from both audiences and critics. Considered by many to be cleverly constructed, wittily written, slightly cynical, and undeniably entertaining, the work contains all the elements that would help establish Coward's reputation as a playwright.

Hay Fever is set in the hall of the Bliss family home. The eccentric Blisses—Judith, a recently retired stage actress, David, a self-absorbed novelist, and their two equally unconventional children—live in a world where reality slides easily into fiction. Upon entering this world, the unfortunate weekend guests—a proper diplomat, a shy flapper, an athletic boxer, and a fashionable sophisticate—are repeatedly thrown into melodramatic scenes wherein their hosts profess emotions and react to situations that do not really exist. The resulting comedic chaos ends only when the tortured visitors tip-toe out the door.

Designed to showcase the larger-than-life personalities of celebrated actors (many of whom were close friends of the playwright), *Hay Fever*, as Coward himself observed in the introduction to the first volume of *Play Parade*, has "no plot at all and remarkably little action. Its general effectiveness therefore depends on expert technique from each and every member of the cast." The play's humor is provided by context. When the show was revived in 1964, Coward remarked upon how the biggest laughs "occur on such lines as 'Go on,' 'No there isn't, is there?' and 'This haddock's disgusting.'... the sort of lines... [that] have to be impeccably delivered." Although Coward claimed that he intended only to amuse and cared little about posterity, he might have been pleased that the simple dialogue in *Hay Fever* would continue to be well-delivered and well-received half a century after it was written.

Author Biography

Noel Peirce Coward—the celebrated actor, composer, and playwright once described as the person who "invented the '20s"—was born on December 16, 1899, in Teddington-on-Thames, Middlesex, England, to Arthur Sabin and Violet Agnes (Veitch) Coward. His father worked as both a clerk for a music publishing company and a piano salesman. Young Noel attended Chapel Royal School in Clapham but learned his most vocational lessons while studying acting with Sir Charles Hawtrey's drama company. Working with this theater group, he developed comic timing and his trademark casual demeanor. Encouraged by his mother, Coward made his first professional theatrical appearance when he was only twelve. He continued to act in London throughout his teens, while also making both his first attempts at playwriting and his film debut in director D. W. Griffith's 1917 feature *Hearts of the World*.

Coward's first play was produced in 1920; three more of his compositions went on the stage in 1922. *The Young Idea* (1922), although deemed a pale imitation of playwright George Bernard Shaw's style, showed signs of the unique humor found in Coward's later work. Already prolific, Coward produced four more plays before writing *Hay Fever* in the three days following his first trip to the United States in the fall of 1924. He wrote seventeen more plays in the next decade, often acting in, directing, producing, and composing music for them as well. During this period he wrote what is widely considered his best work, the comedy *Private Lives* (1930), in which he starred with actress Gertrude Lawrence. Lawrence was only one of the theater luminaries—including Laurence Olivier, Vivien Leigh, John Gielgud, Claudette Colbert, Mary Martin, Tallulah Bankhead, and Michael Redgrave—with whom Coward formed close friendships. Like these celebrities, the playwright cultivated a debonair public persona. He embodied—both on stage and off—the image of the suave, cynical gentleman who appears in evening dress, a cigarette in hand, ready to offer witty cocktail party repartee.

Among his sophisticated theatrical companions it was an "open secret" that Coward was a homosexual, but he never came out publicly. During most of his lifetime the British censors did not allow works containing homosexual themes to appear on stage, and Coward's one play which depicted gay characters, *Semi-monde*, although written in 1926, did not get produced until 1977.

After 1935, Coward wrote twenty more plays, including the hit *Design for Living* (1933) and his biggest box office success *Blithe Spirit* (1941), a comedy of manners that ran for two thousand performances in London and won the New York Drama Critics Circle Award for Best Foreign Play in 1942. After World War II public tastes changed, and Coward's work received less critical attention. Yet, his reputation was well established, and he continued to express his talents in diverse ways: publishing fiction, acting in films, and continuing to write songs, movie scripts, and plays. In 1970, he was honored with a knighthood as well as a special Antionette (Tony) Perry Award. Three years later, on March 26, 1973, he died of a fatal heart attack in Blue Harbor, Jamaica.

Plot Summary

Act I

When the curtain rises, the two adult children of the Bliss household are relaxing in the hall (main living room) of the Bliss family country home. The siblings' conversation reveals that the daughter, Sorel, wishes their family were more normal. She expresses a desire to change, but her brother, Simon, says it is fine to be different. They both observe that their mother, who has recently retired from a successful acting career, has been very restless. They speculate that she might return to the theater. Sorel also announces that she has invited a diplomatist named Richard Greatham down for the weekend.

Their mother, Judith, enters from the garden and says she hopes the housekeeper Clara has prepared the Japanese Room for her guest. The ensuing dialogue reveals that each family member has invited someone for the weekend and they all expected their guests to sleep in that same room. Irritated, each criticizes the others' prospective visitors. David—the father and Judith's husband—enters the room in the midst of this argument. He has come down from his study where he has been writing his latest novel. He casually tells everyone that he invited a young woman for the weekend to observe her behavior, and then heads back upstairs before anyone can say anything.

After David exits, Judith, Sorel, and Simon continue complaining about how awful the weekend is going to be. Soon, however, Judith announces that she has decided to return to the stage and revive one of her most successful plays, *Love's Whirlwind*. Recollecting favorite passages from this drama, she prompts the children to join her in acting out a scene that begins with the cue "Is this a game?" Their reenactment is interrupted when the doorbell rings.

Clara opens the door and lets in Sandy Tyrell, the athletic amateur boxer invited by Judith. The children go upstairs and Sandy and Judith's brief conversation reveals his infatuation with her. The doorbell rings again. This time, Clara admits Simon's guest, Myra Arundel, who greets Judith familiarly before Judith takes Sandy away, leaving the latest arrival to her own devices. Myra strolls around looking very much at home until Simon rushes in. He tries to kiss Myra, but she pushes him away. She continues to rebuff his advances as he expresses his adoration for her.

The bell rings once more, and Clara opens the door for Richard Greatham and Jackie Coryton. Richard asks for Sorel, and Clara goes in search of her. Simon immediately drags Myra outside leaving Richard and Jackie alone to make awkward small-talk until Sorel appears. She sends Jackie up to find David, then sits down with Richard, who expresses his admiration for her unconventionality while she offers similar praise of his propriety.

Clara enters with tea. Simon, Myra, David, and Jackie rejoin Richard and Sorel. The visitors all attempt to begin some polite conversation, but they keep starting sentences at the same time and eventually give up. The scene ends in dead silence.

Act II

After dinner that night all eight main characters are in the hall talking at once, trying to choose a game to play. They decide on "Adverbs," which involves one person leaving the room while the rest choose an adverb. Then the person re-enters and tries to guess the word based on watching the others perform actions in the manner of that adverb. The shouted half-explanations of this enterprise confuse Jackie, but the Blisses begin the game anyway. Sorel goes out. The rest of the group argues over word selection. Richard proposes "winsomely," David "drearily," Judith "saucily," and Myra— under her breath—"rudely." Jackie, who still does not understand the game, suggests "appendicitis."

Judith agrees with Richard that "winsomely" is best and calls Sorel back into the room. Judith performs the first action, handing a flower to Richard in a manner she considers winsome. Myra then attempts to do the next action but is criticized by Judith. They move on to Richard, but Judith stops him midway through because she does not think he is performing well either—and it turns out he had been acting out the wrong adverb. Finally, it is Jackie's turn but she refuses to do anything. Her shy protestations are so sweet and innocent, however, that Sorel guesses the word just as everyone starts yelling at each other. The game breaks up. Simon grabs Jackie's hand and pulls her out in the garden; Sorel drags Sandy into the library; and David takes Myra outside.

Left alone with Richard, Judith begins flirting, inducing him to lean forward and kiss her. She jumps back instantly and dramatically announces that David must be told everything. Confused, Richard listens to Judith go on about how heartbroken poor David will be that she is leaving him to be with her new love (the unwitting Richard). The diplomat tries to protest, but she sends him out into the garden, never letting him finish a sentence.

Judith then opens the library door and stands looking shocked as Sorel and Sandy emerge guiltily, suggesting they have been caught kissing. Switching roles, Judith now loudly laments what a fool she has been. Sorel initially tries to say that "it was nothing" but quickly gives up on this approach and begins playing along, claiming she and Sandy love each other. This allows Judith to nobly "give" Sandy to her daughter before exiting. Once her mother is gone, Sorel clarifies the situation for the befuddled young man, explaining that she knows they do not love each other but she had just said so because "one always plays up to mother in this house; it's sort of an unwritten law."

Sandy and Sorel exit while Myra and David enter talking about the plot of David's latest novel.

As their conversation progresses, Myra confesses that she accepted the weekend invitation in order to meet David because she admires his books. David says that he writes bad novels and wonders if Myra has an ulterior motive in complimenting his work. She then expresses her affection for him, and he respond by asking first whether they should elope and then whether she wants him to make love to her. Offended, she pulls away but is drawn back when he takes her hand and says they can still "have a nice little intrigue." He grabs and kisses her; she resists but then gives in. At this moment, Judith appears and sees them. She immediately launches into the role of wronged wife. David starts out saying Judith is speaking nonsense, but then he begins to play his expected part. Interrupting Myra's protests, he says he and Myra love each other and commends his wife's bravery in the difficult situation.

Just as David and Judith shake hands, Simon rushes in announcing excitedly that he and Jackie are engaged. This news brings Sorel and Simon out of the library and prompts Judith to shift roles again, now acting the part of the bereaved mother anticipating an empty nest. As Jackie tries to deny the engagement, Myra breaks in with a denunciation of the whole family's theatricality. Everyone talks at once as Richard enters and unsuspectingly asks, "Is this a game?" Recognizing the cue, Judith launches into the scene she and the children enacted earlier. Simon and Sorel catch on immediately and speak the appropriate lines. David starts laughing. The four visitors stand watching in absolute bewilderment.

Act III

Act III opens the following morning. A breakfast table has been set up in the hall and Sandy enters, sits and begins eating. He jumps at every sound, however, and when he hears someone approaching he runs into the library. Jackie then enters, takes some food, sits down, and starts to cry. Sandy comes out and the two have a conversation about how uncomfortable they were the night before and how crazy the Blisses are. When they hear people approaching, they both go into the library. Myra and Richard now enter and help themselves to breakfast. Their conversation echoes that of Sandy and Jackie, who subsequently emerge from the library. The entire group decides they are going to return to London. Sandy agrees to drive them in his car. They all go upstairs to collect their things

Judith comes down next, asks Clara for the papers and begins reading aloud the descriptions of herself in the gossip columns. Sorel and Simon enter soon thereafter, followed by David who wants to read them the last chapter of his novel. He begins by describing how his main character drives down one street in Paris to get to a particular plaza. Judith immediately interrupts to say he has the streets wrong and that the one he names does not go where he says it does. This sparks another family argument with everyone talking at once about what streets go where in Paris. As they continue to debate, the four visitors tip-toe down the stairs and out the door. The Blisses only notice their fleeing guests when they hear the door slam. Then after a momentary pause to comment on the guests' rude mode of departure, the Blisses return to their conversation. Judith makes the final statement of the play, announcing she will indeed return to the stage.

Characters

Myra Arundel

Well-dressed, confident, and sophisticated, Myra is invited to the Bliss house by her admirer Simon but coolly rebuffs his advances; her real motive in accepting the weekend invitation is to meet his novelist father, David. Before Myra even appears on stage, Simon's mother, Judith, describes her as a "self-conscious vampire" who "goes about using Sex as a shrimping net." So the audience is not surprised when Myra later begins a flirtatious conversation with David. Myra herself, however, is taken quite off-guard when David asks her directly, "Would you like me to make love to you?" and then refuses to believe that she is offended by the question, saying simply "You've been trying to make me—all the evening."

Although David will not play the game of subtle seduction in the typical manner that Myra expects, he does readily join in the game his wife instigates, pretending that they are ready to break up their marriage so he can be with Myra. Used to being the one who manipulates such situations, Myra is utterly frustrated by the way the entire family's odd behavior takes events out of her control. Towards the end of the play, she angrily denounces the Blisses in a statement which accurately sums up their way of life: "You haven't got one sincere or genuine feeling among the lot of you—you're artificial to the point of lunacy."

David Bliss

David, Judith's husband and Simon and Sorel's father, is an absent-minded writer, wrapped up in his latest book. Although his works—which have titles like *The Sinful Woman* and *Broken Reeds* —are popular, he admits that they are actually "very bad novels." Less melodramatic than his flamboyant wife, David nevertheless is equally self-involved and self-obsessed. He forgets he invited Jackie and, as she reports, rudely greets her by saying "Who the hell are you?" He behaves in a similarly unconventional way with Myra. At first bluntly calling her attempts to seduce him exactly what they are, he ruins the mood with his directness. Then, changing his attitude and willingly participating in the romantic "intrigue," he explains that he loves "to see things as they are first, and then pretend they're what they're not." He again demonstrates this inclination when he calls Judith's wronged wife routine "nonsense" initially, but then—after calling things "as they are"—goes on to "pretend they're what they're not" by joining in the scene and acting as if he does love Myra. At the end of the play, his self-absorption is emphasized once more as he reads the last section of his new novel to the family and debates with them over the streets described in a certain passage, not noticing the departing guests.

Judith Bliss

Judith is David's wife and Simon and Sorel's mother. A well-known stage actress who has temporarily retired, she made her name in melodramatic plays with names like *Love's Whirlwind* and *The Bold Deceiver*, which she admits were not that good even though the public loved them. Bored with everyday life, she amuses herself by acting out exaggerated roles and theatrically misinterpreting ordinary situations. During the course of the play, she takes on the demeanor of the rural lady of the manor, the long-suffering mother, the glamorous star, the flirtatious coquette, the betrayed lover, and the wronged wife, among others. Vibrant and eccentric, she is unable to keep from slipping into dramatic personae constantly, and her family has learned to adapt to and play along with this tendency. She is also in the habit of bolstering her ego by inviting young male fans to the house and refuses to apologize for it, telling her daughter not to think that the younger woman has "the complete monopoly of any amorous adventure there may be about."

Judith's whims and inclinations dictate the action in many of the play's scenes, her dominant personality overshadowing those that are more quiet and conventional. Her every action supports her self-descriptive statement, "I won't stagnate as long as there's breath left in my body." Early on she tells her children, "I long for excitement and glamour," and the rest of the play shows her ability to create her own excitement when the world does not provide enough for her.

Simon Bliss

Simon is Judith and David's adult son. He first appears on stage looking disheveled and unwashed, and, like the rest of his family, he seems to care little about other people's opinions. In contrast to his sister, he has no desire to reform the Blisses' unconventional and often inconsiderate ways, remarking, "we see things differently, I suppose, and if people don't like it they must lump it." In typical Bliss fashion, Simon is given to extremes: expressing energetically his adoration for the worldly Myra one minute, then seducing the innocent Jackie the next.

Media Adaptations

- A videorecording titled *Hay Fever: A High British Comedy* was produced by the George Washington University (Washington, DC) Department of Theatre and Dance in 1995. It is available on two VHS videocassettes running 110 minutes. This college production was directed by Nathan Garner and features the actors Carole Stover, John F. Degen, Maura Miller, Brian Coleman, Kristiana Knight, Alan Goy, Kerry Washington, Michael Laurino, and Rachel Flehinger.

- Another videorecorded production of *Hay Fever* is included on tape number seven of the Theater Department Productions 1989 VHS video series from Seton Hill College in Greensburg, Pennsylvania.

- A sound recording of a radio play adaption of *Hay Fever* featuring actors Peggy Ashcroft, Tony Britten, Millicent Martin, Julia Foster, and Maurice Denham is included in the 1988 British Broadcasting Corporation Enterprises audio collection entitled *A Noel Coward Double Bill*. These two analog cassettes run 180 minutes and also contain a sound recording of *Private Lives*. The tapes were distributed in the United States by the Novato, California-based Mind's Eye Co.

- The Radio Yesteryear company of Sandy Hook, Connecticut, released a sound recording of *Hay Fever* featuring actors Everett Sloan and Ann Burr. First broadcast as a radio play on June 3, 1947, this audio version was released in 1986 as volume forty-six of the Radiobook series.

- Although *Hay Fever* has yet to be adapted into a feature film, at least seventeen of Coward's other plays and screenplays were made into movies between 1927 and 1987, including a 1946 British production of *Blithe Spirit* directed by David Lean, and a 1931 Hollywood version of *Private Lives* directed by Sidney Franklin and starring Norma Shearer and Robert Montgomery. Additionally, Coward acted in at least twelve films, including director Richard Quine's *Paris—When it Sizzles*, a 1931 feature starring Audrey Hepburn. A complete Coward filmography is available in the Internet Movie Database at http://us.imdb.com.

He shocks poor Jackie when he kisses her in the garden and then rushes into the house to announce their engagement, even though she has never agreed to marry him. He also willingly participates in his mother's theatrical scenes—both scripted and improvisational—just as his father and sister do. His own artistic inclinations tend toward drawing, and in the final act he brings a new sketch down to show the others.

Sorel Bliss

Sorel is Judith and David's adult daughter. She is the only member of the Bliss family who expresses any concern about their unorthodox behavior. At the start of the play she laments to her brother that they are all "so awfully bad-mannered" and "never attempt to look after people" and are essentially "abnormal," observations that will be clearly proven true in the scenes to follow. Sorel, however, is "trying to be better," and so invites a man for the weekend whose perfectly proper behavior is the antithesis of the Blisses' wildly inappropriate actions.

Sorel's attempts at reform are only party successful, however, as the audience sees when she still regularly takes part in her mother's impromptu dramas. Although she does not truly have deep feelings for Sandy, she pretends she does so her mother can act the part of a betrayed lover who nobly gives away the man she loves. Sandy gets swept up in the moment and confesses his love for Sorel, but she clarifies the situation, telling him, "I was only playing up—one always plays up to mother in this house; it's sort of an unwritten law."

This confession shows a change in Sorel's habits; as she tells Sandy further, "A month ago, I should have let you go on believing that, but now I can't— I'm bent on improving myself." Despite her attempts at self-improvement, Sorel remains very much a Bliss: eccentric and unconventional. At the end of the play she and her family are absorbed in their argument about the trivial details of David's novel, oblivious to the departure of the tormented weekend guests.

Clara

Described in the stage directions as "a hot, round, untidy little woman," Clara is a long-suffering Bliss family employee. Originally Judith's dresser at the theater, she is now the over-taxed family housekeeper. Clara must deal with the imposition of four unexpected weekend guests all by herself because the maid is home sick with a toothache.

Jackie Coryton

Jackie is the "perfectly sweet flapper" David has invited for the weekend because "she's an abject fool but a useful type" and he wants "to study her a little in domestic surroundings." Described in the stage directions as "small and shingled, with an ingenuous manner," she is shy and ill at ease from the start. She feels awkward making small-talk with Richard when the two are left alone early in the play. Later she is completely confused and embarrassed by the word game but in her embarrassment acts out "winsomely"—i.e. sweetly and innocently—so well that Sorel still guesses the adverb. She has no idea what to do when Simon suddenly announces their engagement. By the next morning she is so distraught that she bursts into tears when sitting alone at the breakfast table. Completely distressed, she concludes at the end of Act III that the Blisses are "all mad," and is as eager as her fellow visitors to escape from the house.

Richard Greatham

Richard is the "frightfully well-known diplomatist" Sorel has invited for the weekend. Described in the stage directions as "iron-gray and tall," his instinct for politeness is revealed in his first moments on stage when he manages to keep up some sort of conversation with the shy Jackie while they wait in the hall. Although Sorel admires him precisely because of his conventional manners, he is drawn to her and her family because they are "so alive and vital and different from other people." He admires Judith's vitality and says he feels "dead" by comparison, but he hardly knows how to respond when after one brief kiss she leaps up and begins announcing plans to leave her husband. Later, when he comes in from the garden to encounter a chaotic scene he unwittingly speaks the line, "Is this a game?" that is the cue for Judith and the kids to launch into the scene from *Love's Whirlwind*.

Sandy Tyrell

Sandy is the amateur boxer Judith has invited for the weekend. In her words, he is "a perfect darling, and madly in love with me." But as Sorel says to her, he is just another one of the "silly, callow young men who are infatuated by your name." Described in the stage directions as "fresh-looking" with an unspoiled, youthful sense of honor and rather big hands, owing to a "misplaced enthusiasm for boxing," Sandy has an athletic form that contrasts with Simon's less-developed physique. Having fallen in love with Judith when he saw her on stage, Sandy at first can't believe his good fortune in being her houseguest. He is soon disillusioned, however, by the discovery that she has a husband. Later when he kisses Sorel in the library and is discovered by her mother, he gets swept up in Judith's interpretation of events—that Sorel has stolen him away from Judith—until Sorel admits that it was all just another act. Such strange encounters with the Blisses leave him so unnerved that the next morning he hides in the library when he thinks one of them might be about to enter the room.

Absurdity

Much of the humor in *Hay Fever* derives from the way Coward's characters, despite being placed in ordinary situations, behave in odd and unexpected ways. These eccentricities make typical interactions seem ridiculous to the viewer. The Bliss family leaps to melodramatic and emotional extremes at the slightest provocation, leaving their guests at a loss for how to respond and highlighting the absurdity of social and romantic conventions that might otherwise be accepted as normal. While Coward's exploration of this theme was primarily in the service of entertainment, there are also elements of social criticism in his mocking of conformity.

Culture Clash

Although the characters in *Hay Fever* (save Clara) belong to the British upper class, they can still be divided into two separate groups, each reflecting a different worldview or "culture." The four members of the Bliss family follow their own unique rules for personal interaction, rules that allow them to slip into fictional roles and act out melodramatic plots whenever the mood strikes them. The four weekend visitors, contrastingly, follow the conventional rules that instruct people to act according to their "real" social roles, behaving in a polite and predictable manner even if this means denying their genuine inclinations or feelings. These two cultures clash over the course of the weekend visit, resulting in the abundance of silly situations that amuse the audience.

Topics for Further Study

- Several critics have commented upon the strong connections between *Hay Fever* and Edward Albee's 1962 play *Who's Afraid of Virginia Woolf?* Compare and contrast these two works, considering how each playwright takes a similar situation and setting and develops it to very different effect.

- Both Coward as an individual and the plays he wrote are often associated with 1920s "Bohemian" culture. Research the meaning and evolution of the term "Bohemian" in early twentieth-century western culture. Once you have a good sense of what the term means, consider whether it accurately describes the worldview of Coward and his characters.

- In addition to being a playwright, Coward was a talented composer and lyricist. Locate and listen to some recordings of Coward's songs. Then consider how the lyrics and melodies of the music relate to the theme and tone of *Hay Fever*.

- More so than some artists, Coward is considered to have revealed facets of his personality in his plays. Research Coward's biography— including both his public persona and his private existence as a closeted homosexual—and then consider the question of how his comedies, including *Hay Fever*, might be seen to reflect his character and/or life experience.

Family

In this play, the members of the Bliss family have problematic relationships with outsiders, yet they are able to interact contentedly—if oddly—

among themselves. In a reversal of the typical family drama plot, none of the potential romantic connections with their weekend visitors are able to rival or disrupt familial bonds; a fact that is clearly illustrated in the final scene when the four Blisses sit around the breakfast table absorbed in their own idiosyncratic conversation while their guests slip out unnoticed.

Illusion vs. Reality

The line between illusion and reality is constantly crossed in the Bliss household. Elements of theater and fiction are freely integrated into everyday life as family conversations slide into dialogue from a play or family members begin to act out melodramatic emotions they do not genuinely feel. But Coward also reveals—through the small deceptions of the "normal" visiting characters—that the "real" world is just as full of play-acting as the Bliss world—only people accept these everyday illusions in the name of good manners and social convention.

Individualism

The unusual beliefs and behavior of the Bliss family, which confound their guests and amuse the audience, also reflect an individualistic ideology that celebrates people who rebel against the restraining conventions of society at large. Each Bliss is a unique individual and follows his or her inclinations without considering the opinion of others. Being a homosexual, Coward was particularly sensitive to the narrow definitions of "normal" that society placed on people. His celebration of the Blisses' individuality can be read as a veiled criticism of such prescriptive social mores.

Dialogue

Coward was one of the first playwrights of his generation to use naturalistic dialogue, that is, to have his characters speak in the same ordinary phrases that people use in everyday conversation. Earlier dramatists had employed an epigrammatic style, wherein the actors on stage spoke in quotable "epigrams," complex and witty phrases that sound poetic or literary. By contrast, Coward's plays rely on the interaction between charismatic performers to grab attention and the context of a given line to generate laughs. Viewers might not leave the theater quoting a single clever phrase, however, chances are they laughed their way through the actual performance because of the amusing situations depicted on stage.

Comedy of Manners

In a comedy of manners, humor and interest derive from social interaction and conversation rather than from elaborate or suspenseful plots. Jane Austen's novels and Oscar Wilde's plays, for example, can both be categorized as comedies of manners. *Hay Fever*, with its focus on a series of amusing situations that all take place in one upper class home, is a sophisticated and irreverent adaptation of this comedic form.

Farce

Hay Fever employs many elements of farce, a comic theatrical form in which exaggerated characters find themselves in improbable situations and engage in wordplay and physical humor intended to provoke simple hearty laughter from the audience. Although Coward's play carries a bit more social weight than a traditional farce, it does make use of farcical word games and broadly drawn characters.

Irony

Many of the humorous comments made by the members of the Bliss family are good examples of dramatic irony. This type of irony comes from situations where the impact of a line or action depends upon the audience being aware of something the character is not. So for example, it is ironic, and therefore funny, when David—who both accepts unusual behavior from his family and behaves quite unconventionally himself—reacts to his guests' surreptitious departure by saying "People really do behave in the most extraordinary manner these days." Although the audience is aware of how David's comment actually describes his own behavior, David himself does not see this and so makes his observation free of self-reflection.

Juxtaposition

Throughout the play, Coward juxtaposes the

carefree unconventional Blisses with their anxious, convention-bound guests. Each new pairing of characters provides an amusing contrast between one of the self-absorbed impulsive family members and an uneasy, confused visitor. These oppositions —both of personality types and personal expectations—produce much of the work's humor.

Pace

The success of a Coward comedy depends upon the live production maintaining a fast pace. The humor and impact of a play like *Hay Fever* comes partly from the rapid staccato dialogue, the type of syncopated speedy delivery of lines that would later become the hallmark of late-twentieth-century plays by writers like David Mamet (*Glengarry Glen Ross*).

Romantic Comedy

Coward generates a good deal of humor by disrupting the audience's expectations regarding the traditional plot of the romantic comedy, which is usually a story of a love affair between two people who must overcome obstacles before they can marry—or at least end the play in a happy conclusion. As *Hay Fever* opens, the viewer might expect a plot in which a series of mismatched couples swap partners in order to find happier pairings—in other words the typical romantic comedy plot multiplied by four. Yet Coward thwarts such expectations, making fun of the familiar storylines about illicit love and adulterous spouses during the course of the play and in the end leaving all the members of the Bliss family just as they were when the play started.

Satire

Satire is a type of humorous critique used in both fiction and drama to ridicule political or social philosophies. *Hay Fever*, with its depiction of self-absorbed bohemian artists and their misguided conventional admirers, can be seen as a gentle satire of the excesses both of pretentious creative people and of the adoring public who indulge such egotistical behavior because these people are famous. This has come to be known as the "cult of personality" or "cult of celebrity," in which famous people are so revered that they are above social reproach.

Historical Context

In the 1920s, Great Britain experienced political upheaval resulting from the first global war, as well as social transformations resulting from industrialization. Technological innovations also significantly altered the era's cultural landscape. Both the optimism and the anxieties induced by such extreme changes were reflected in the period's art and literature.

Before World War I (1914-1918) there was great optimism in Europe about the future of parliamentary government. After the war, political attitudes were very different. After witnessing both the war's terrible death toll and the perpetual chaos in Postwar continental legislatures, Europeans were more likely to question government action and demand social justice. For Britain in particular, events early in the century underscored the government's vulnerability. The Easter Rising in Dublin (1916), the granting of Irish Independence (1921), and the shootings in India that started Mahatma Ghandi's peace movement (1919), all indicated that the British Empire was no longer invincible.

Meanwhile, unrest on the European continent set in motion events that would culminate in a second world war. The Bolshevik Revolution took place in Russia in 1917. Benito Mussolini assumed dictatorial power in Italy in 1922. Germany, struggling under the burden of World War I reparation payments, experienced rapid inflation of its currency in 1923-24, resulting in worthless money and a demoralized populace. Finding support from a dissatisfied German citizenry, Adolf Hitler reorganized the New Socialist or "Nazi" party and published the first volume of his manifesto, *Mein Kampf*, in 1925; his rise to power in the next decade would set the stage for World War II.

The first World War also altered the international economic order. In 1914, most of Europe's economies depended on Great Britain and Germany. By the time the fighting stopped in 1918, the United States had become the main economic power. In the period between the wars, England would have to adapt to industrialized modes of production—factories that used assembly lines and electric power—and the resulting loss of jobs. The country suffered severe unemployment, with as many as two million people out of work in 1921-1922 and still a million unemployed in 1925. A lot of these people had lost coal mining jobs, and the miners would go on to lead a massive protest, known as the General Strike in 1926. These events augured the world economic crisis of 1929-1932 (a global event that manifested itself as the Great Depression in America).

Despite its economic difficulties, the British government had to meet the Postwar expectations of its people, who demanded more social services and greater civil rights. In the early-twentieth century, English legislative acts reflected changing perceptions of the rights of workers and the role of women. The 1911 National Insurance Act established some medical coverage and unemployment benefits for workers, while the 1925 Pensions Act set aside retirement funds for them. World War I brought many women into the national workforce, making them less dependent on male wage-earners and more willing to assert their property rights. Although the Divorce Bill (1902) and Female Enfranchisement Bill (1907) had taken some steps to empower women, significant changes only came after the war. It was not until 1918 that British women who met age and property requirements got the vote.

During the following decade women continued to agitate for full suffrage, which was finally won in 1928. Many of those involved in the suffrage debate were dubbed "New Women," women associated— both positively and negatively—with personal independence, unconventional attitudes, and less-restrictive fashions. The image of the high-spirited "flapper" wearing loose-waisted dresses with skirts above the knee was often equated with this newly liberated female role.

The daily life and attitudes of all British people changed a great deal in the first decades of the twentieth century. Rapid urbanization took the majority of citizens away from the country. By 1911, 80% of the population of England and Wales lived in urban areas. Despite periods of crisis, there was a general rise in the standard of living. This increase in national income allowed people to spend more on luxuries; the demand for non-essential goods went up accordingly. There was also a great increase in literacy as school attendance became mandatory across Europe.

Compare & Contrast

- **1925:** It is the height of the modernist period in literature, numerous books later considered classics are published. These works include Theodore Dreiser's *An American Tragedy*, Willa Cather's *The Professor's House*, T. S. Eliot's *The Hollow Men*, F. Scott Fitzgerald's *The Great Gatsby*, Ernest Hemingway's *In Our Time*, Gertrude Stein's *The Making of Americans*, and Virginia Woolf's *Mrs. Dalloway*. The 1925 Pulitzer Prize for fiction goes to Edna Ferber for her novel *So Big*.

  Today: Recent British and American books that have earned praise include Alice McDermott's novel about ill-fated romance and family deception, *Charming Billy*, which won the National Book Award; Ian McEwan's exploration of personal intrigue and public humiliation, *Amsterdam*, winner of the Booker Prize; Phillip Roth's examination of a father-daughter relationship in the turbulent 1960s, *American Pastoral*, honored with the Pulitzer Prize for fiction; and Rafi Zabor's uniquely humorous story about a talking saxophone-playing animal, *The Bear Comes Home*, which received the PEN/Faulkner Award for fiction.

- **1925:** The Charleston—a jittery, kinetic dance performed with a partner to music with a staccato, syncopated 4/4 rhythm gains great popularity. Although originating in Charleston, South Carolina, the dance soon became an international trend and, along with flappers, became emblematic of the "Jazz Age" of the mid-1920s.

  Today: After two decades in which rock and rap music dominated popular music, a revival of swing music and dancing is taking place in many parts of America and Europe. Partner dancing—including the lindy-hop, a variation on the Charleston developed in the 1930s—has made a comeback with American youth, and remakes of big band swing tunes are appearing on the top-ten record charts.

- **1925:** American writer Anita Loos

publishes *Gentlemen Prefer Blondes*, which was made into a film in 1928. This popular novel's main character, Lorelei Lee, provides the prototype for the caricature of the "dumb blonde" that would resurface in many books, shows, and movies throughout the second half of the century; beginning in the late-1950s, film star Marilyn Monroe would come to epitomize the dumb blonde.

Today: In the latest variation on this theme, writer/director Tom DiCillo's 1998 independent film *The Real Blonde*, starring Matthew Modine, Daryl Hannah, and Catherine Keener, offers a witty critique of the cultural ideal of feminine beauty and the "dumb blonde" stereotype. Modern culture has mostly abandoned the dumb blonde stereotype, though it does occasionally reappear.

- **1925:** Nellie Taylor Ross is elected governor of Wyoming, the first woman to be elected to such a post in the United States. Margaret Thatcher, who later became Britain's first woman Prime Minister (in 1975), is born this same year.

Today: Although the number of female politicians still does not begin to adequately represent the number of female voters in either America or Europe, women continue to be elected and appointed to high office. In 1993, for example, Janet Reno was appointed the first female Attorney General of the United States, and in 1998 she became the first person in the modern era to hold the post for more than five years; serving in the same Clinton presidential cabinet, Madeleine Allbright becomes the first female secretary of state in 1997.

Thanks to innovations in communications media, even those no longer in school had greater access to all kinds of information. Radio and cinema became significant political and cultural influences. Right before the war the British silent film industry was thriving; there were six hundred cinemas in Greater London in 1913. After 1918, Hollywood-left largely unaffected by the fighting—dominated film production. Although Europeans like Sergei Eisenstein made great artistic innovations in the field, the United States industry had the money to produce costly extravaganzas like *Ben Hur* (1926) and establish world-wide stars such as Charlie Chaplin, who was, ironically, British.

The first American radio broadcast took place in 1920, the first British in 1922, inaugurating an era of mass persuasion. In the years between the two world wars, cinema, radio, and microphones became powerful communication tools manipulated by monolithic fascist and communist parties to incite public responses. Dictators used propaganda films and large public meetings to inspire the same kind of hero-worship elicited by movie stars.

All these developments created great hopes as well as great fears, both of which were articulated by the period's artists. The modern writers of the 1920s—including Americans F. Scott Fitzgerald (*The Great Gatsby*) and Ernest Hemingway (*For Whom the Bell Tolls*) and Britons James Joyce (*Ulysses*) and Virginia Woolf (*To the Lighthouse*)— broke with traditional novel form, emphasizing individual thought and expressing the alienation felt by the Postwar generation. Visual artists—such as the European painters Wassily Kandinsky, Paul Klee, Henri Matisse, and Pablo Picasso—also experimented with new techniques, developing the non-representational forms of abstraction and cubism.

At the same time aesthetic movements like Art Deco, a popular style in 1920s furniture, clothing and architecture, optimistically embraced modern materials and designs. A similarly positive tone carried through the music of composers such as Aaron Copland and George Gershwin. Although the era Fitzgerald dubbed the "Jazz Age" and W. H. Auden called the "Age of Anxiety" was marked by a loss of faith in society, the incredible creative output of the time shows a continuing faith in the power of art.

Critical Overview

Throughout his career, Coward was generally praised as a skillful dramatist capable of constructing well-balanced comedies filled with natural-sounding dialogue and broadly humorous situations. Even those who criticized his work as being too trivial and lacking in deep meaning have usually acknowledged his plays as entertaining, which is precisely what Coward intended them to be. Today the playwright's critical reputation rests largely on his comedies of manners written between the two World Wars, works—including *Hay Fever* —that capture the sophisticated, irreverent and high-spirited mood of 1920s elite society.

When *Hay Fever* premiered in 1925, some critics like James Agate, the reviewer for London's *Sunday Times*, complained that the play offered neither a useful moral nor admirable personalities. As Agate wrote, "There is neither health nor cleanness about any of Mr. Coward's characters, who are still the same vicious babies sprawling upon the floor of their unwholesome creche." Yet even this critic had to acknowledge that "it would be foolish to insist upon attacking this play on the score of truth or morality.... As a piece of brilliant, impudent, and sustained fooling the play is very pleasant entertainment." The 1925 critical consensus supported this final observation, that *Hay Fever*, though certainly not educational, was undeniably entertaining.

Many of Coward's contemporaries underestimated the extent to which the play would continue to appeal to later generations of theatergoers. Some thought the casual dialogue would rapidly become dated. While others, like Agate, anticipated that the play would only be favored by a "purely Metropolitan audience." Yet such predictions have proved false. *Hay Fever* is still frequently performed for late-twentieth century audiences. In professional revivals, as well as community and college theater productions, its jokes remain fresh, garnering laughs from a wide range of viewers. Audiences today seem to agree with the assessment expressed by Coward's fellow writer W. Somerset Maugham in his introduction to the 1929 collection *Bitter Sweet and Other Plays*, that *Hay Fever* is a "masterpiece in miniature."

In the past three decades, productions of the play have consistently earned critical praise. In 1965, Penelope Gilliatt complimented a version of *Hay Fever* "immaculately revived by the author" himself. Writing for *Harper's* in 1982, John Lahr expressed his view that *Hay Fever* is "Coward's finest light comedy." A 1985 production elicited similarly positive reviews. Clive Barnes, in the *New York Post*, noted that this brilliant revival of Coward's play reclaimed the playwright's "reputation as a major twentieth-century playwright" and gave the work the "patina of a classic." Although Frank Rich may have complained in his 1985 *New York Times* review that *Hay Fever* has "skin-deep characters, little plot, no emotional weight or redeeming social value and very few lines that sound funny out of context," like many critics before him he acknowledged that it was "unlikely" that the audience would "stop laughing and start thinking" long enough to notice. By contrast, Jack Kroll argued in *Newsweek* that this "timeless comedy of ill manners" actually "isn't superficial," but rather "it's *about* superficiality."

Literary historians now rank *Hay Fever* among Coward's most enduring works. In 1964, A. C. Ward in his *Twentieth-Century English Literature, 1901-1960* identified it as a "first-rate comedy." While in 1996, Jean Cothia in her *English Drama of the Early Modern Period, 1890-1940* expressed the generally agreed upon scholarly view that "where Coward makes his continuing claim to attention is in his wonderfully symmetrical comedies of egoism, desire and bad manners: *Hay Fever* (1925), *Private Lives* (1931), and *Blithe Spirit* (1941)."

Starting in the 1970s, some critics also began to place Coward's works in the context of the homosexual literary tradition. When Coward died in 1973 near the time when a famous gay producer, Hugh Beaumont, also passed away, one columnist in the *Spectator* wrote that although the two men's deaths did not mean "the whole edifice of homosexual domination of the British theatre will come tumbling down," the "loss of these two pillars" does make the "structure ... look a little less secure."

But in the succeeding decades, gay issues and identity—in the theater as in the rest of society— were more freely acknowledged.

In the increasingly less restrictive academic world of the 1980s and 1990s, critics have begun to explore possible homosexual themes and perspectives in Coward's comedies, observing how plays like *Hay Fever* mock heterosexual romance, allow characters to form unorthodox connections, and generally flaunt conventions of all kinds. Lahr, in his 1982 book *Coward the Playwright*, even went so far as to argue that Coward has an "essentially homosexual vision."

The main reason Coward's reputation remains secure at the end of the twentieth century, however, seems to be that the sophisticated humor of well-crafted plays like *Hay Fever* still provide the sort of light entertainment that pleases audiences. As Cothia observed, when "performed with panache by a team of actors ... skilled in delivery of the well-bred insults and discourteous frankness that characterize the staccato dialogue," Coward's comedies "are works that perceive the absurdities of sexual relationship and social organization," allowing us to gently laugh at ourselves.

What Do I Read Next?

- *The Collected Short Stories*, a 1962 collection that brings together all of Coward's short fiction. Like his better plays, the author's short stories showcase his skill with wordplay and considerable wit.

- Poems by Dorothy Parker, an American contemporary of Coward's. Her work also captures much of the same irreverent wit and high energy that defined the 1920s artistic world in which they both circulated. Two notable collections are *Enough Rope* and *Death and Taxes*.

- *Private Lives*, Coward's 1929 comedy about a divorced couple who meet again when both are honeymooning with new spouses. As in *Hay Fever*, the main characters' behavior befuddles and confuses their new spouses. Some consider this to be Coward's best play.

- *Pygmalion*, a play by influential British playwright George Bernard Shaw. The story deals with the transformation of a lower-class woman to fit upper-class ideals; it was later adapted into the popular stage musical and film *My Fair Lady*.

- *Quicksand*, Nella Larsen's 1928 novel depicts the "Roaring '20s" from another perspective, that of a black woman trying to negotiate her racial identity as she travels between Europe and America.

- *Who's Afraid of Virginia Woolf?*, a 1962 award-winning play by Edward Albee that is much indebted to *Hay Fever* for its dramatic situation of a married couple tormenting guests who do not understand the familial tensions and deceptions that are being played out in front of the them. Unlike Coward's play, however, Albee's work also deals with a deeper theme of marital discord.

Sources

Agate, James. Review of *Hay Fever* reprinted in *Red Letter Nights*, Jonathan Cape, 1944, pp. 240-42.

Barnes, Clive. "For Rosemary Harris—Love & Gesundheit!" in the *New York Post*, December 13, 1985.

Cothia, Jean. "Noel Coward" in her *English Drama of the Early Modern Period, 1890-1940*, Longman, 1996, pp. 101-02.

Coward, Noel. Introduction to *Three Plays*, Benn, 1925, pp. viii-ix.

Coward, Noel. Introduction to *Play Parade*, Vol. I, Doubleday, Doran, 1933.

Gilliatt, Penelope. "Coward Revived" in her *Unholy Fools: Wits, Comics, Disturbers of the Peace: Film and Theater*, Viking, 1973, pp. 242-43.

Innes, Christopher. "Noel Coward (1899-1973): Comedy as Social Image" in his *Modern British Drama, 1890-1990*, Cambridge University Press, 1992, pp. 238-60.

Kroll, Jack. "Serving up the Guests" in *Newsweek*, Vol. 106, no.26, December 23, 1985, p. 77.

Lahr, John. *Coward the Playwright*, Methuen, 1982, pp. 66-68.

Lahr, John. "The Politics of Charm" in *Harper's*, Vol. 265, no. 1589, October, 1982, pp. 64-68.

Maugham, W. Somerset. Introduction to *Bitter Sweet and Other Plays*, Doubleday, 1928, pp. v-xiii.

Rich, Frank. "'Hay Fever,' Noel Coward Comedy" in the *New York Times*, December 13, 1985, p. C3.

Ward, A. C. *Twentieth-Century English Literature 1901-1960*, Methuen University Paperbacks, 1964, pp. 131-32.

Waspe, Will. "A World Suddenly Less Gay" in the *Spectator*, March 31, 1973, pp. 399-400.

Further Reading

Coward, Noel. *Present Indicative*, Doubleday, 1937.

> This first volume of Coward's autobiography covers his youth and early career up to 1931.

Hoare, Philip. *Noel Coward: A Biography*, University of Chicago Press, 1998.

> This well-researched biography of Coward offers a good balance of insight into his private life and discussion of his literary works.

Payne, Graham, with Barry Day. *My Life with Noel Coward*, Applause Theater Books, 1997.

> This memoir by Coward's longtime companion provides both a detailed personal portrait of the playwright and excerpts from his previously unpublished writings.

Payne, Graham, and Sheidan Morley, editors. *The Noel Coward Diaries*, Little, Brown, 1982.

> Although clearly written with publication in mind, these diaries give the reader further examples of Coward's sophisticated wit and unconventional opinions.

9 781375 381093